# "MISPLACED FAITH"

# "MISPLACED FAITH"

## Dr. R. Michael Baldock

Library of Congress Control Number:        2021909867

PAPERBACK:              978-1-955347-63-1
EBOOK:                  978-1-955347-64-8

All scripture used is from the King James Version of the Bible unless otherwise noted. All Hebrew and Greek definitions were from the New Strong's Expanded, Exhaustive Concordance of the Bible.

**Ordering Information:**

For orders and inquiries, please contact:
1-888-404-1388
www.goldtouchpress.com
book.orders@goldtouchpress.com

Printed in the United States of America

# CONTENTS

# INTRODUCTION

In my many years of ministry I have without a doubt studied more on the subject of **"faith,"** than any other. Just the subject of faith has been intriguing to me. After all, I have preached for many years to believe in God (the Father) which cannot be seen (in His person) with the natural eye. Then also to believe in Jesus Christ (the Son) who lived and died to save mankind from their sin and to top it all off, the Baptism in the Holy Ghost.

None of this really makes any sense to the natural man. However, we are not just natural but we are also spiritual. Man is made a triune being. We are *"body, soul and spirit.* The only true way of understanding any of this, is by **'Faith.'** And the only way to please God is walking by faith (Hebrews 11:6).

I have been in this faith walk over fifty years. Not only do I believe by faith, I am convinced by faith, I am persuaded by faith. With this being said it makes perfect sense to continue to dig and study so we may understand faith. There are some questions concerning faith that we need to discover;

1. **Where it comes from?**

2. **How to receive faith?**

**3. What kind of Faith do I need?**

**4. How to walk in it and walk in correct faith?**

**5. What happens when I find myself walking in 'Misplaced Faith.'**

Within this particular study in this **"Faith Series"** I want to identify just what **"Misplaced Faith"** is, and how to correct it. Putting together this series on faith has been a joy and delight. I have been blessed by putting this together, although it really isn't (wasn't) me. It has all been done under the leadership of the Holy Spirit without which this study could have never been

While gathering notes on top of notes, researching and reading whatever I could get my hands on concerning faith, I was amazed during this study to find growth within me, concerning my personal walk of faith. My hope and prayer is that within the following pages there will be w revelation that will create a deeper faith walk for you. As I said earlier, the only way to please God is by faith. And, the only way to God (contrary to some teaching in the modern day church) **is through Jesus Christ and what He finished at Calvary (The Cross) this and this alone must be the object of our faith! (Heb. 12:2**

# CHAPTER 1

# "What is Misplaced Faith?"

### *'Misplaced Faith Defined'*

On the sixth day, God created the greatest of all His creation, He created man in His own image and likeness; male and female. He blessed them and gave them the ability to be fruitful, and to multiply, and to replenish the earth. He gave them dominion over all the inhabitants of the earth. God gave them every herb bearing seed, and every tree yielding seed for meat with the exception of the Tree of Knowledge of Good and Evil. His command was;

> **"But of the Tree of the Knowledge of Good and Evil, you shall not eat of it for in the day that you eat thereof you shall surely die. Gen. 2:17**

The day came when Eve was approached by the serpent, who, was being used by Satan. He said to Eve;

> *"Now the serpent was more subtle than any*
> *beast of the field which the Lord God had made.*
> *And he said unto the woman, Yes, has God said,*
> *You shall not eat of every tree of the Garden?"*

> *"And the woman said unto the serpent, We may*
> *eat of the trees of the Garden."*

> *"But of the fruit of the tree which is in the midst*
> *of the garden, God said, You shall not eat of it,*
> *neither shall you touch it, lest you die." Gen. 3:1-3*

In Eve's response she added to what God had spoken to Adam. God never said, *'neither shall you touch the tree.'* Any time we add too or take away from what God has spoken we become vulnerable to the onslaught of the enemy. Notice in verses 4 and 5 the endless pursuit of the serpent to deceive Eve. Satan outright denies the Word of God before Eve.

When Eve saw that the tree was good for food, and it was pleasant to her eyes, she partook of it and gave Adam some and he did eat. This was the very beginning of the three temptations; *"the lust of the flesh, lust of the eyes, and the pride of life."* Even from these, one cannot excuse Adam. While Eve was deceived and submitted to temptation Adam was not. He blatantly disregarded what God had spoken to Him. Adam's sin was not partaking of the tree of Knowledge of Good and Evil. Adam's sin was due to unbelief; he just did not believe what God had said to him. It was his unbelief that led to his disobedience. This was the beginning of **'Misplaced Faith!'** Adam placed his faith within his own strength, ability and knowledge. This is amazing considering the time that Adam spent with God. Nobody knows how long it was from the time Adam was created until he fell. The reason being, Adam was created an eternal so there was no need for time.

The feeble attempt of Adam and Eve sewing together fig leaves and making themselves aprons in order to cover their nakedness (sin) was insufficient at best. It is like the sinner of toady who tries to cover themselves with, self made morality and religious practices. Again, this was because of Adam **'Misplacing his Faith!'**

## God Reveals What Must Be the Object of Faith!

## The Promise of the Cross and the Finished Work of Jesus Christ!

*"And I will put enmity (animosity) between you and the woman (presents the Lord now "You used the woman to bring down the human race, and I will use the woman as an instrument to bring the Redeemer into the world, Who will save human race), and between your seed (mankind which follows Satan) and her Seed (the Lord Jesus Christ); it (Christ) shall bruise your head (the Victory that Jesus won at the Cross [Col. 2:14-15]), and you shall bruise His Heel (the sufferings of the Cross). Gen. 3:15*

*The Expositor's Study Bible Jimmy Swaggart*

*"Unto Adam also and to his wife did the Lord God make coats of skins, and clothed them (in the making of coats of skins, God, in effect, was*

*telling Adam and Eve that their fig leaves were insufficient; as well, He was teaching them that without the shedding of blood, which pertained to the animals that gave their lives, which were a Type of Christ, is no remission of sin; in this first sacrifice was laid the foundation of the entirety the Plan of God as it regards Redemption; also, it must be noticed that this is the "Lord God" Who furnished these coats, and not man himself; this tells us that Salvation is altogether of God and not at all of man; the Life of Christ given on the Cross, and given as our Substitute, provides the only covering for sin; everything else must be rejected). Gen. 3:21*

*Expositor's Study Bible Jimmy Swaggart*

From this time forward, the object of man's faith had to be focused on the coming Messiah, Jesus Christ and what He would accomplish on the Cross. While waiting on the coming Christ there had to be blood sacrifices made of animals. Even though these sacrifices could not deliver man nor take care of his sin problem. Yet, these sacrifices pointed to the Supreme Sacrifice and that being Jesus Christ (Hebrews 10:1-18)!

Within the Old Testament there are several occasions where man **'Misplaced their Faith.'** The first such occasion happened with the sacrifice of Cain. Cain offered as a sacrifice the fruit of the ground to offer unto God. Cain was very much aware of the type of Sacrifice That God would accept, instead, he rebelled and was demanding God to accept the labor of his own works, which God would not nor could not accept. It was Abel who offered the Sacrifice that was more excellent (Hebrews 11:4).

Another occasion where there was, *'Misplaced Faith'* was when the children of Israel grew impatient with Moses and decided to collect their gold and make a *'Golden Calf'* to worship (Exodus 32:1-10). Again, the children Israel misplaced their faith when they could entered into the Promised Land of Canaan, instead, ten of the spies sent into the land brought back an evil report. It was Joshua and Caleb who kept their faith focused on the correct object. (Numbers 13:17-33).

The list goes on and on for those in the Old Testament who at one time or another, *'Misplaced their Faith!*

For today's believer, the correct object of faith must be in and only in *'The Cross and the Finished Work of Jesus Christ!'*

*This is the 'Faith' that pleases*
*God and the only 'Faith' He will accept!*

# CHAPTER 2

# "O ye of little faith"

The above phrase, *"O ye of little faith"* was spoken by Jesus Christ and it is recorded five times in the New Testament (King James Version). One time it was spoken directly to Peter and the other four times Jesus spoke it toward the twelve disciples. This phrase appears four times in the Gospel of Matthew and one time in The Gospel According to Luke.

It seems that Jesus was the only person to use this phrase. This phrase cannot be found by Greek grammarians in their secular literature. Three centuries following the New Testament, Patristic authors used this phrase. However, it was only used in the sense in which Jesus Christ introduced it by the phrase, *"little Faith."*

It is interesting to note, that when Jesus spoke concerning, *"lack o f faith"* which is from the Greek word, *"apistos"* meaning, faithless. He used it with a sternness which was due to those who rejected Him. In Greek grammar, when there is an **'a'** applied to the front of the word it nullifies or speaks in a negative sense. For an example, the word, *"pistos"* means, the faithful. When the letter 'a' is applied it becomes, *"apistos"* meaning faithless, having no faith. This would explain when Jesus said, *"O ye of little faith,"* He used as a more tender, mild rebuke in contrast to when He used the phrase, *"lack of faith."* This is because the latter deals with unbelief, which will always slam shut the door to God and all His blessings.

*"O ye of little faith,"* deals with the opportunity for a person to enlarge and become stronger in faith. I personal believe that Jesus used this term with His disciples as a teaching tool. This will come into a greater focus in the following chapters. Let's examine this phrase for a greater understanding. *"O ye of little faith"* originates from the Greek word, *"Oligopistos"* which is a compound word. *"Oligos"* meaning, little, small, brief or puny (in extent, degree, number, duration, value) al-most, brief, briefly, few (a) little. The second word, *"Pistos"* means, believing faith, a reliance upon Jesus Christ for salvation and a constancy in such profession (Hebrews 10:23)

Together we have the word, *"Oligopistos"* meaning, to have little faith, trusting to little, insufficient faith, lacking full confidence and or trust in Jesus Christ. It comes with the idea of one beginning in faith an losing sight of it i.e. *"Misplaced Faith."* It is one putting their faith within the wrong means and source.

The greatest (in my opinion) show of *"Misplaced Faith,"* is when we put our faithful trust in our own abilities, strengths and knowledge. This creates nothing but disaster. There are four major areas that occurred that brought the response, *"O ye of little faith,"* from Jesus. I said earlier, I am convinced that Jesus used these four opportunities as a teaching tool. The lessons that He taught were not only to reveal insufficient brief faith, but also I have seen so many people, (believers) fall victim to small, puny, and brief insufficient faith. Their walk started out great and then the cares of this life caught their attention over where their faith was to be and remain. I heard a great quote years ago concerning remaining in faith (being faithful). *"The key to remaining in faith is to be the same before a storm, in the middle of a storm and at the end of the storm."* This is what I want to address in the following chapters.

It can be so easy to get caught up in the distractions (and there are many) of everyday living. I am reminded about the *"Parable of the Sower,"* which is recorded Matthew 13:3-9; Mark 4:3-9; Luke 8:5-15.Within this great parable is the lesson of how to handle and keep the word once it has been sown into your life. A parable is a comparison illustration used to reveal and explain a truth. It begins with by sowing seed (the Word of God)

1. **Seeds (the Word of God) were sown and some fell by the way side. And the fowls (demonic powers) came and devoured them.** If Satan could have his way, every time the Word of God is sown, through teaching, preaching, exhortation, and or a song, he would do whatever it would take to keep the believer from hearing and receiving. Have you been in a church service and while the praise and worship or the teaching and preaching of the Word is coming forth, there comes some kind of distraction? Often times, it becomes difficult to get your mind back where it should be, **"On the Word."** Little demons, Satan's imps, will try anything and everything to keep the Word of God from flourishing in the believer.

2.  **More seed (Word of God) was sown and it fell on stony places, which had little ground. When the seed came up and when the sun was up, they were scorched because they did not have any root (deepness) and they were withered away.** Herein is another tactic that the enemy can use. Without a firm Gospel under our feet making for a firm foundation (root) when problems arise (the scorching sun) what Word one may have is withered without any production.

3.  **More seeds sown and fell among Thorns and the thorns grew and choked out the seed.** Here is another situation where the Word was sown and had little if no growth. Once again, this reveals how we can get so caught up with the cares of this life that they steal away any production from the Word. One of the best ways to thwart this is it to renew our minds daily (Romans 12:2). We also need to learn to bring our thoughts in line with the Word (2 Corinthians 10:3-7) and learn how to think on correct things (Philippians 4:8)

4.  **More seed was sown and this time it was sown upon good ground and brought back a harvest, some as hundredfold, some sixtyfold and some thirtyfold.** The *"good ground"* spoken of here, is those who are receptive to the Word being, taught, preached, exhorted, sang and or read. It is the attention that we give to the Word of God that results in a harvest. I know before I teach or preach I pray this prayer, *"Lord anoint our ears to hear, our minds to comprehend and our hearts to be receptive."* I strongly believe that not only does the speaker need to be under the anointing, but, also

those who are in attendance. The anointing will destroy any operation Satan would use to block any harvest the Word will bring. Also as hearers of the Word we need to keep our ground (ears, mind, hearts) good at all times.

5. **Notice how Jesus followed this parable:** *"Who hath ears to hear, let him hear."* The *"hearer"* has total responsibility to take care of and put to use the Word that is being sown into them. It is also important to notice in this parable that only about one-fourth do much at all with the Word sown where about three-fourths fail. Look at our history and also the **"Modern day Church"** and these statistics bear the truth of the examples displayed in this great parable.

You may be thinking, *"What does this have to do with faith?"* Great question; For the Word to work and produce in one's life it has to be by faith. We can only receive faith by the word (Romans 10:17). We can only live an operate in the Faith that God supplies (Romans 12:3) which comes upon receiving Jesus Christ as Lord and Savior. Also, true faith is revealed by the works one does (James 2:10-26). We cannot even please God without faith (Hebrews 11:6). Last but certainly not least, we are ton continually look to Jesus who is the *"Author and finisher of faith)*

In this faith series we have touched on, *"What Faith is, A Pilgrims Faith, The Heroes of Faith, Faith Being Tested, Great Faith, Fight the Good Fight of Faith and The Faith."* All of these studies have been designed not only to teach on faith, but how to have the correct object of faith and remain faithful. This has to be the everyday challenge for each of us!

# CHAPTER 3

# Anxiety (worry) Verses Faith

*"No man can serve two masters: for either he will hate the one, and love the other; or else he will hold to the one, and despise the other. Ye cannot serve God and mammon." Matthew 6:24*

Within the above passage, *"No man can serve two masters."* Jesus addresses one of the greatest dilemmas that can be seen within the modern day Church and hundreds if not thousands of Christians. This great dilemma is revealed by many trying to hold onto the hand of God while still holding onto the hand of the world.

*"No man can serve two masters"*

The word serve is one of importance. It is written in *"The Present Infinitive"* which refers to continuous or repeated action, without implying anything about the time of action.

There must come a time in the life of the believer to let go of anything that takes (distracts) him/her from serving God to its fullest. It is totally impossible to serve two masters. We must decide who we will extend faith too. When anxiety (worry) becomes a controlling factor in one's life, it will derail them from living a life of faith in what Jesus Christ accomplished at Calvary!

## *"Ye cannot serve God and mammon."*

The word serve (while it is grammatically the same as the first word serve) takes a deeper meaning. It is from the Greek word, *"Douleuo"* meaning, servant. To be in the position of a servant and act accordingly; to be subject and serve in subjection, bondage: It also come from the Greek word, *"Doulos"* meaning; a slave, one who is in permanent relation of servitude to another, his will altogether consumed in the will of another. Therefore, one's serving cannot be divided.

The word *"mammon"* is an interesting word. Over the years I have heard this word taught as being *"money, filthy lucre,"* which has an element of truth. However, it goes far deeper than money. This word is derived from the Babylonian word *"mimma"* meaning, anything at all. So, it is not limited to money but anything that comes between a person and God. In this context we are going to deal with, *"Anxiety, Worry"* which is a faith killer. Jesus stresses the believer to avoid that which one should not get caught up in. worry.

> *"Therfore I say unto you, Take no thought for your life, What ye shall eat, or what ye shall drink; nor yet for your body, what ye shall put on. Is not life more than meat, and the body than raiment?"*

1.  **Take No Thought For Your Life.** This phrase is actually referring to what Jesus said in verses 19-21 concerning where our treasures are. *"For where your treasure is, there will your heart be also."* The phrase, *"take no thought for your life"* is a tough saying. It refers directly to what we eat, drink, and what we clothe ourselves with. Jesus was certainly not suggesting that we go without these things, nor are we to ignore them. However, He was putting a demand on what the real priorities of life are to be. Notice the question that Jesus asked and how He puts an emphasis on the priorities of life.

    > *Is not the life more than meat, and the body than raiment?"*

Certainly, life has a great value within what we eat, drink and on our bodies. Turning one's life over to Jesus Christ and allowing Him to be the Lord and Savior is, of the utmost importance. Can we add eternal life in Christ through worry? NO! God's care of our eternal life was made known by His giving of Jesus Christ and He becoming the Supreme Sacrifice that all who believe (put their hope, trust, confidence and faith) will have Eternal and Abundant life. See John 3:16 and John 10:10. You will see this unfold as we dig a little deeper. Jesus reveals that these things are provided by God and is something that one should not covet nor worry about.

> *"Behold the fowls of the air: for they sow not, neither do they reap, nor gather into barns; yet your heavenly Father feedth them. Are ye not much better than they?"*

13

2. **Which Of You By Taking Thought Can Add One Cubit Unto His Stature?** Certainly the believer is to be aware and give due diligence, in business and the supplies that are needed. However, those things (the afore mentioned things) must not take a priority over the things of God!

> *"And who of you by worrying and being anxious can add one unit of measure (cubit) to his stature or to the span of his life?" Matthew 6:27 Amplified Bible (See also Psalm 39:5-7)*

The question here is; "Will worry (anxiety) help you to grow taller, be stronger or add one day to how long you will live?"

3. **And Why Take Ye Thought (Worry or Have Anxiety) For Raiment?** In relieving oneself of worry/anxiety of what we will wear, Jesus gives the following examples;

   A. <u>**Consider the lilies of the field;**</u>

      a. How they grow

      b. They toil not

      c. Neither do they spin

   B. <u>**Solomon, in all his glory (magnificence, excellence, dignity and grace) was not clothed like the lily of the field.**</u>

   C. <u>**God clothed the grass of the field**</u>

   D. <u>**Surely He (God) will clothe you!**</u>

Once again I want to emphasize in no way is the scripture saying or teaching that a person should not take care of themselves. However, it is teaching, where our faith should be and what the priority of one's life should be. Jesus follows this question and statement by saying;

*"O ye of little (oligopistos, brief, little puny, insufficient faith."* In other words, "**Why have misplaced your faith?**"

4. **Take no thought (worry/anxiety) about what you will eat, drink or be clothed with.** Within the statement, Jesus gives clarity to why He used these examples;

    A. **The Gentiles, here are used in the context of those who do not know God and are outsiders to the Nation of Israel.** Being on the outside looking in prevents one from being a partaker of promises from God!

    B. **God is aware that the believer has need of all the necessities of our everyday living. And He alone is the God of provision (Jehovah Jire)**

    C. **The Priority of The Believer.**

        *"Seek first the kingdom of God and His righteousness."*

        *"But seek for (aim at and strive after) first of all His kingdom, and His righteousness His way of doing and being right] and then all these things taken together will be given you besides.*

5. **Take No Thought (worry/anxiety For Tomorrow.** I have discovered in my own life that worrying about what will

or will not take place tomorrow is a waste of time and energy. Please understand, I am in no way suggesting that we should not make plans and provisions for tomorrow (the future). What I am saying is, it is certainly not faith that consumes itself with what or what may not happen, nor does it worry about the things that are out of our control. Peace for today and the following days are contingent on where we put our faith. Correct faith is placing all our faith upon Jesus Christ and what He accomplished at Calvary. This kind of faith is sufficient not only for today but all the days that are ahead. Each day brings with it a new adventure and even some difficulties. When all of your faith, hope, trust and confidence is in the right place (Jesus Christ and the cross) what happens today and or tomorrow, every difficult situation can be (will be) minimized!

On a personal note;

In my many years of ministry without a doubt there have been times when I **'Misplaced my Faith!'** Probably, more times, than I care to remember. However, there are just a couple, I want to share with you.

In the late seventies I was doing evangelistic work. One thing that I have never done in all the years of my ministry was charge a church a certain amount for me to come and minister the Word. Well, times were tough and offerings were small to say the least. I was in a revival in a certain city. Things were going well as far as the moving of the Holy Ghost. However, each night the offerings were barely enough for me to by my gas back and forth, not to mention, putting food on our table and paying bills. I was having a really tough day. It was difficult for me to get ready for the service that night. When it was about the time for me to minister the Word, a banner on the back wall of the pulpit had a quote from David;

> *"I have been young, and now am old; yet have I not seen the righteous forsaken nor his seed begging bread." Psalm 37:25*

For some untold reason, that passage of struck a wrong cord in me. Here I was without two nickels to rub together, the offerings were extremely low, I was having trouble getting together enough gas to get to church. Let me say, none of those things were in any way an excuse for my actions that followed. I had always considered myself having total faith, trust and confidence in God. I was about to be shaken to the core. When I got with very little money it hit me and I mean it hit me hard. I was so angry with God. When I went into my bedroom I tossed my Bible on the bed, it bounced and fell to the other side of the bed. I begin to throw one more, immature baby fit. I told God His promises did not work and I was not going to preach ever again. I e nerve to tell God even had that I never wanted Him to speak to me again. After this however long tirade, there was a still small voice that spoke these words to me. *"After I tell you want I want to say, if you so choose I'll never speak to you again."* My response was, *"Okay."* God then said; *"I LOVE YOU!"* I said, *"But, I don't want You to love me."* Then man, I broke down and began to cry which seemed like a river of tears. Of course, I began to repent with everything that was within me. Wow! I sure learned a very valuable lesson that night. I learned what *'Misplace my Faith'* was even though at the time I did not realize that was what I had done. It took me years to realize that I had fallen from my faith. But, thank God, in His loving mercy and kindness He picked me up dusted me off and continued to this day to anoint me to preach this great gospel.

Another occasion where I allowed my '**Faith to get Misplaced,**' (I certainly knew better this time), my family and I relocated to another state on the promise of me taking a paid position in the church leadership. We were also promised free housing with all water, electrical and gas bills paid for an entire year. We had not been there but a few months and things were not going as promised (planned). We tried to buy a house only to have it block by the enemy (not saying who the enemy used). We finally found a house with great rent on an acre lot. I helped set up a college site at the church. The college was from entry level though the doctorate program. I soon found out my position, it was teaching three college classes a week for a very minimal broken. I found myself hanging by a thread. It was taking a mental toll on ,me and depression soon set in, which was something that I had battle all of my life but I thought I had defeated it, I was wrong. The mental and spiritual toll it was taking on me through me into a deep spin. No, I never left God, this time I never blamed God, I knew, exactly where the blame landed.

After facing this situation for about six years, God opened up a door for us to move back home to Indiana. We had been gone from home for about eighteen years. Even though I was glad to make this move, for the next year and a half I was still not in the greatest mental and spiritual condition. While having a problem forgiving myself for falling into what seemed like a trap and battling depression again, the Holy Spirit awakened me one morning to SBN (at the time I was not aware of this channel) there I heard Brother Jimmy Swaggart and a panel discussing and teaching on the **'Message of the Cross.'** My first thought was, I know about the Cross and what Jesus Christ did there, and then the Holy Spirit ask me, *"Do you really?"* I'm thinking, I have preached about the Cross all of my ministry, then the Holy Spirit admonished me to listen. Listen, I did, and what I heard and researched over the next couple of weeks changed me completely. **The depression left my spiritual being was restored and now I am closer to God than ever! PRAISE GOD!**

It was a hard way to learn, but thank God for the revelation of the **'Cross and the Finished Work of Jesus Christ!' I am not the same man I used to be and I am still learning daily about the 'Cross and what Jesus Christ accomplished there.'**

<u>**DON'T EVER ALLOW YOUR FAITH TO GET MISPLACED!**</u>

# CHAPTER 4

# Fear (The Fear of Harm) Verses Faith

### Facing Storms Part 1

*"And He saith unto them, Why are ye so fearful, O ye of little faith? Then He arose, rebuked the winds and the sea; and there was a great calm.."*
*Matthew 8:26*

There is something to be said about how we handle the storms of life. This is part one of two in which we will deal with the disciples while facing a storm.

The Bible references storms or bad weather over sixty times. In forty of those sixty times the scripture uses a comparison of storms and the life we live. It is important to understand that no matter how close to God one may walk, they are not exempt from a storm. The importance in facing the storms of life is how we navigate through them.

In this passage of scripture we are going to examine the extreme between fear and the calm. Notice the following verse;

> *"Now when Jesus saw the great multitude about Him, He gave commandment to depart unto the other side." verse 18*

This is following on the heels of Jesus healing Peter's mother-in-law, along with casting out demonic spirits, and healing all that were sick just by **"His Word!"** We need to keep in mind **(the casting out of evils spirits and healing the sick by His Word!)** as go further in this chapter.

Now the *"command,"* is given to depart to the other side. There are two elements in this command that I want to point out.

1. **They were leaving where great miracles had taken place.**

2. **The *"other side"* was not a great place.**

The other side was across the Sea of Galilee into the country of the Gergesenes and where they would be entering was a place full of tombs and inhabited by those who were possessed by demonic spirits. Why would anyone want to go there? I am sure that that question arose within the minds of the disciples. The truth is, Jesus knew exactly why they were traveling there and there was a lesson to be learned while going.

When Jesus commanded them to depart to the other side it meant that no matter what they might face while on the sea they had a guarantee they would get there. When we follow the direction of the Holy Spirit in our daily walk we will arrive in the place He wants us to be.

I am not certain that the disciples were at ease with this entire situation, which is evident in the following.

> *"And, behold, there arose a great tempest in the sea, insomuch that the ship was covered with the waves: but He (Jesus) was asleep."*

> *"And His disciples came to Him and awoke Him, saying Lord save us: we perish." verse 24-25*

Mark recorded the disciples saying; *"Master, carest thou not that we perish?" Mark 4:38b*

Their boat was being filled with water and was tossed by the winds. All of this going on while Jesus was in the hinder part of the ship asleep. The cry of the disciples was one of fear and feeling as if Jesus did not care about what was going on nor care about their safety. The fact was, since Jesus was aboard the disciples probably did not anticipate this ever happening.

The phrase, *"But He was asleep"* reveals a couple of things to us.

1.  There was no doubt that Christ was tired after the healings and deliverances that He had done just prior to entering the ship.

2.  Jesus being asleep also reveals the peace inside Him in the midst of the storm.

3. This was going to be a teaching tool for the disciples. Surely, they knew that the Son of God was not nor could not be killed in this manner.

The disciple then awoke Jesus saying, *"Lord, save us: we perish."* I truly believe at this point the disciples had exhausted all of their strength, ability and knowledge to combat the storm. After all, they had faced many storms out on the sea while fishing. But this storm was so intense and out of their control. Could it be, as a last resort they cried out to Jesus for help? That is what a lot of people do. They wait until they couldn't figure it out and they exhausted all of their own efforts, then they called out to Jesus for help.

Upon calling out to Jesus for help, Jesus responded saying;

> *"Why are ye so fearful, O ye of little (misplaced) faith? Then He arose, and rebuked the sea; and there arose a great calm" verse 26 Emphasis Mine*

The real question is, *"Why would the disciples be in fear while Jesus was on board with them?"* Did they think because He (Jesus) was on board with them that a storm of any kind would not come?

Over the years I have heard many preachers/teachers proclaim, if we are living in the right place in correct relationship and fellowship with God, these kinds of situations just will not happen. That is so far from the truth and do not be deceived by such teaching. Some even teach that when the disciples cried out; *"We perish"* they were expressing a bad, doubtful, negative confession. That would be laughable, if it wasn't so sad and hadn't created havoc in so many lives.

Have you ever felt like you are out on life's sea and being tossed by a storm and you are all alone? I am sure at one time or another that has happened. The storms of life can be devastating at times both naturally and spiritually. It may feel like Jesus is asleep of maybe that He doesn't care about your situation, But, He does! Keep this in mind

> *"And we know that all things work together for good to them that love God, to them who are called according to His purpose." Romans 8:28*

The key to the above verse is, **"And we know."** These three words are of the utmost importance when facing any kind of storm in life. The sad fact is, many do not know nor understand that God will be in the middle of their mess, working out His plan and purpose!

As stated earlier, no one is exempt from the storms of life, naturally and spiritually.

1. **From the beginning of time there have been storms.**

2. **The scriptures give warnings of storms coming, in the forms of, afflictions, tribulations, troubles, trials and despair.**

3. **Just like the weather storms also come in many ways; Thunderstorms, Hail storms, Ice storms, Tornadoes, Rain, Floods, Hurricanes and others.**

4.  Sometimes storms come without any warning and catch us unaware (unprepared).

**"And We Know!"** There must be an understanding to why we even have to face storms.

1.  Understand that storms are a part of our lives.

2.  Understand that storms come to us for a reason. Most often they are times of teaching and revealing.

3.  Understand the opposition that is in the storm (your adversary) so you can successfully make it through with victory.

4.  Understand what to do and how to respond while in a storm.

5.  Understand (discern) what type of storm and where it is coming from!

### Remember, Every Storm Has A Purpose

1.  They give us direction (a new direction or a redirection)!

2.  They inspect us! They cause us to look deep within and discover where we are at in our walk of faith.

3.  They correct us! They help us see what is wrong and how to correct it.

4. **They connect us! They create a deeper connection with the "Cross and The Finished Work of Jesus Christ!"**

## "And We Know!"

*"These things I have spoken unto you, that in me ye might have peace. In the world ye shall have tribulation: but be of good cheer; I have overcome the world." John 16:33*

It really does not matter what type of storm you are facing. Keeping your faith in Jesus Christ and His Finished Work at Calvary guarantees you and me "**VICTORY!**"

# CHAPTER 5

# "Doubt Verses Faith"

### Facing Storms Part 2

When I was a child I was never fearful of a storm (I am still not fearful). I can remember when I was about ten years old watching a tornado passing through a field by our house. I was fascinated by what I saw. Since that time I have not only seen my fair share of storms but I have been in the middle of many storms both physically and spiritually.

I remember a time when myself and a few friends when deep sea fishing in the Atlantic Ocean. We had traveled several miles out into the deep and while fishing there arose a storm. The storm clouds had engulfed us along with rain. It became so bad that it was difficult to see anyone on board of the boat. The boat was being tossed about by the waves of the ocean like a small bobber on a fishing line. I must admit, I was a little troubled however, I was not fearful. I knew or I thought surely this will pass soon.

Life can be looked at as a huge ocean with storms erupting on a regular basis. We can be likened as ships traveling on this vast ocean of life. There will be (and are) times when we will face rough and angry storms. It is how we prepare for the storms and how we respond to them that will make us or break us. Do we focus on the storm or the blessings that can come from the storm?

In this chapter we are going to examine another storm that the disciples found themselves in.

> *"And straightway Jesus constrained his disciples to get into a ship, and to go before him unto the other side, while He sent the multitudes away."*
> *Matthew 14:212*

As we get started, let me remind you that this was following a great miracle of the feeding of five thousand men, besides the women and children with two fishes and five loaves. Not only did they all eat, they ate until they were all full and the disciples still gathered twelve baskets full of the leftovers. How soon the disciples would forget this great feat.

The word, **"constrained"** is an important word to have a clear understanding of and which I believe to be the mental state of the disciples. The word means; to compel, to force by external violence by an authoritative command. Looking at that meaning causes me to think that the disciples probably could see storm clouds gathering and didn't think it was a good idea to be on the water at such a time as this.

Another great point is noticing what Jesus said to them while putting them in the ship, *"to get in the ship, and to go before*

*Him unto the other side."* Since Jesus said, *"to go before Him unto the other side,"* meant, no matter what they would face on their journey they would arrive on the other side safely. I learned something concerning this many years ago and have said it times over. Often times, I know in my life, God speaks to leave point **A** and go to point **B** without giving much if any information concerning the traveling from point to point. I have come to realize that when God says leave one place and go unto another that it is not my concern what comes up in my path, **"I will make it to where He is sending me!"**

As I have stated earlier, it is not the storms in life that stop us, it is how we respond to them. When talking about people who have been in some of the most severe storms there is something for all of us to learn. I believe that every storm has within it a valuable lesson. When facing a storm it is those who remain calm as possible and not panic that make better decisions and come away unscathed. To become knowledgeable and effective in a storm is vital to your health naturally and spiritually. How we handle the storms of life can bring devastation or blessing.

There is a purpose in every storm;

1. **In Genesis chapters 6-8 the purpose of the greatest rainfall of all time, was to "Purify and Cleanse the Earth!"**

2. **The storm that Jonah found himself in was to "Redirect and Refocus!" It certainly was a I time for this prophet to examine the road he was traveling.**

3. **The storm that the disciples faced in the previous chapter was to remind them to always "Trust in God's Word and have faith in His help!"**

4. **Psalm 107 reveals that when storms come and everything is seemingly out of control, "God is Still in Control!"**

I do believe that God uses the storms in our lives as a learning tool and to bring blessings. The storm you may be facing is not meant to destroy you but for you to see the **"Hand of God"** in the middle of that raging storm and hear Him say, **"Peace, Be Still!"** Now, let's dig a little deeper into what the disciples were facing and just how they handled this particular storm.

> *"And when He (Jesus) had sent the multitudes away, He went apart to pray: and when the evening was come, He was there alone."*
>
> *"But the ship was now in the midst of the sea, tossed with waves: for the wind was contrary."*
> *Matthew 14:23-24*

This is where everything takes a little turn and gets very interesting. Don't forget, the great miracle of feeding the five thousand had just taken place. There are some lessons to learn notice;

1. **Jesus put them in the storm;** This I believe, is a reminder that we can be in the **"Perfect Will of God"** and still get caught in a storm. Storms do not just come to those walking in disobedience to the Word or those doing something

wrong. They also come to those living a life directed by the Holy Spirit.

2. **Jesus was totally mindful of their situation and was watching over them.** *"And He (Jesus) saw them toiling in rowing; for the wind was contrary unto them: and about the fourth watch (somewhere between 3 a.m. and 6 a.m.) of the night he cometh unto them, walking upon the sea, and would have passed by them." Mark 6:48*

There are a few things to take notice of here;

    A. **Jesus was mindful of them at all times which included their situation.**

    B. **Jesus was watching over them.**

    C. **He (Jesus) often watches to see how we respond to the storm and then He gets involved.** This serves as a reminder when David said; *"The Lord is my shepherd and I shall not want." Psalm 23:1*

3. **Jesus will always show up in your storm.** This is where I think the story takes on a turn that needs to be noticed. *"And when the disciples saw Him walking on the sea, they were troubled saying, It is a spirit; and they cried out for fear."* Matthew 14:26

The disciples were so overwhelmed by the storm they were in that they failed to recognize who it was walking toward them. This was due to allowing what was happening on, on the outside to dictate what was happening on the inside of them. If we are not careful, we too, can get so caught up with our surroundings that it becomes difficult to see **"The Cross and the Finished Work of Jesus Christ!"** Jesus Christ always shows up just in time.

A. <u>He (Jesus Christ) knows what you and I can handle and what our limitations are.</u>      See, 1 Corinthians 10:13

B. <u>Storms can certainly be unpleasant unless, we find comfort and safety in Him.</u> See Psalm 91

C. <u>The result of being in a storm often times is manifested in a miracle.</u> God is waiting on you to turn your faith back to him and Him alone.

4. <u>There are opportunities that arise while in your storm.</u>

> *"But straightway, Jesus spoke unto them, saying, Be of good cheer it is I"*

> *"And Peter answered Him and said, Lord if it be thou, bid me come unto thee on the water.""And He (Jesus) said come. And when Peter was come down out of the ship, he walked on the water, to go to Jesus." Matthew 14:27-28*

There are several lessons here to learn that will create **"Spiritual Growth!"** Notice; that when Peter got out of the ship the storm was still raging.

A. Storms can and will often reveal the things we need to allow the Holy Spirit to work on in our lives.

   a.) Our weaknesses

   b.) Our character

B. Peter received a revelation that changed his life forever.

C. Revelation will cause you to leave your comport zone. I t will get you out of the boat!

D. At this point, Peter was no longer focusing on the storm but upon the spoken Word "Come" which was leading him directly to Jesus.

5. Jesus (the Word) will see you through every storm;

   *"But when he saw the wind boisterous (strong), he was afraid; and beginning to sink, he cried, saying, Lord, save me."*

   *"And immediately Jesus stretched forth His hand, and caught him saying, O thou of little faith, wherefore didst thou doubt?"*

   *"And when they were come into the ship, the wind ceased." Matthew 14:30-32*

There are many things to learn from these verses;

A. Peter was doing fine until he took his eyes (his faith) off of Jesus and started looking upon the wind (the storm). Any time we take our eyes (faith) off of the Word of God and focus on the surrounding circumstances we get into trouble. Understand, I am in no way saying that we are to go through life pretending that negative circumstances do not surround us at times. What I am saying, is, we are never to allow our focus to be on what is happening around us, but ,our focus (our object of faith) is to always be on the **"Cross and the Finished Work of Jesus Christ."** For it is He and He alone that can save us from our despair.

B. Peter's failure in his faith was evident when he began to sink. However, did you notice, that even though Peter's focus was not on (in) Jesus, Jesus never at anytime took His eyes off of Peter?

C. Even when we make mistakes in our walk or when we feel that we are at wits end and we are sinking into life's storms, Jesus Christ is always there to lift us up again. Peter did do one thing right while being in **"Little Faith. (oligopistis)"** He cried out, saying *"LORD SAVE ME!"* Immediately, without hesitation, Jesus stretched forth His hand and caught him. All it takes for Jesus to pull us out of what seems like a hopeless situation is to cry out and make Him the **"Object"** of our faith.

There may be times when you find yourself in, small, brief, little insufficient or puny in situations. When those times arise, change your focus (object of faith) and watch Jesus stretch forth

His hand and lift you out of those situations (circumstances). Keep in mind the following;

> *"Looking unto Jesus the author and finisher of our faith; who for the joy that was et before Him endured the cross, despising the shame, and is set down at the right hand of the throne of God."*
> *Hebrews 12:2*

4.  What Jesus Christ accomplished at Calvary (The Cross) and His resurrection was, and still is, Him stretching out His hand to immediately save you from the drowning of life's sea.

5.  When Jesus and Peter arrived back into the ship, the wind ceased and the storm dissipated. Again, once the object of your faith becomes correct you will find yourself safely in the hands of Jesus Christ. (see Psalm 91). His grace is all sufficient, **(2 Corinthians 12:9)**

**Are you facing a storm today?**

**Are you feeling like you are in an impossible situation and feel as if you are sinking?**

**If So;**

**Change from focusing on the surrounding Storm and fix your eyes (faith) on the Cross and what Jesus Christ accomplished there.**

**Now, you can begin to embrace the "BLESSING IN YOUR STORM!."**

# CHAPTER 6

# Reasoning Verses Faith

*"Which when Jesus perceived, He said unto
them, O ye of little faith,
why reason ye among yourselves, because ye
have no bread"*
*Matthew 16:8*

This is the fourth time that Jesus used the phrase, *"O ye of little faith."* This was brought about by the disciples, *"reasoning"* among themselves. On the surface, one may ask, *"What was so terribly wrong with them reasoning among themselves?"* This, is will be what we will are discover in this chapter.

Like all the times before, the disciples had just been part of another miracle, the feeding of four thousand with seven loaves and a few little fishes. When everyone was full they (the disciples) gathered seven baskets full of leftovers.

Jesus had just got done addressing the Pharisees and Sadducees concerning signs of the times. Jesus then turns His attention to

His disciples with a great lesson which caused them to reason among themselves.

> *"And when His disciples were come to the other side, they had forgotten to take bread.*
>
> *"Then Jesus said unto them, Take heed and beware of the leaven of the Pharisees and the Sadducees" Matthew 16:5-6*

Jesus was saying, befuddled the disciples so they began to reason among themselves. They came to the conclusion that this was all due to them forgetting to bring bread.

> *"And the reasoned among themselves saying, It is because we have forgotten bread." Matthew 16:7*

The word phrase, *"They reasoned among themselves"* is from the Greek word, *"Dianoema"* which is from, *"dianoeo"* meaning to agitate in mind, and from, *"dia"* denoting separation, and *"noeo"* meaning to think; a thought; reflection.

The disciples began trying to separate and think about what Jesus said. The problem here is, they were trying to reason in their minds something Spiritual and it was not making sense to them, so, they settled (came in agreement) it must be because we did not bring any bread. This would make logical sense seeing that Jesus was speaking of leaven. They were certainly lacking in Spiritual knowledge of the Word Jesus spoke.

By the disciples reasoning that this was all because they had not brought any bread reveals that they were thinking naturally which blinded them to the Spiritual. In my teaching over the years I have discovered this kind of mindset among many Christian believers. It is a gross mistake to try and reason in our natural mind what the Holy Spirit is speaking. When we try to understand the scriptures without the guidance of the Holy Spirit we will find ourselves in error, trying to make sense out of something that we have no clear revelation of.

> *"Which when Jesus perceived, He said unto them, O ye of little faith, why reason ye among yourselves, because ye have not brought bread?"*

It was evident that the disciples had not received the real revelation of Jesus feeding the five thousand and the four thousand. Every miracle that Jesus ever did was not just to take care of a natural situation but also a spiritual one. A great example is found in Matthew 9: 1-6 where Jesus spoke to the man who was sick with palsy;

> *"And behold, they brought to Him a man sick of the palsy, lying on a bed: Jesus seeing their faith said unto the sick of palsy; Son, be of good cheer; thy sins be forgiven thee."*

There were certain scribes (while reasoning among themselves) who came to the conclusion that this was blasphemy. Here again, we find some people trying to reason within their natural minds something that is Spiritual. Jesus responded to their thinking (reasoning).

> *"And Jesus knowing their thoughts said, Wherefore think ye evil in your hearts?"*
> *"For whether is easier, to say, Thy sins be forgiven thee; or to say, Arise, and walk?"*

This is like so many who put Jesus Christ in a box when the prophet Isaiah said,

> *"But He was wounded for our transgressions, He was bruised for our iniquities: the chastisement of our peace was upon Him; and with His (Jesus Christ) stripes we are healed." Isaiah 53:5*

And the apostle Peter saying;

> *"Whose own self bare our sins in his own body on the tree, that we, being dead to sins, should live unto righteousness: by His stripes ye were healed." 1 Peter 2:24*

It is pitiful when the first thing a person thinks of when they hear; *"With His Stripes We are Healed"* is physical first. The true healing that took place and is still in place is that of a *"Spiritual Healing."* Yes, it does pertain to physical healing, however, that is not the primary thing spoken of. The restoration of an intimate relationship with God is the primary focus.

With that being said, it brings the realization that the disciples were missing something in their conclusion. This is the reason why Jesus said, *"O ye of little faith."* Their minds were glued to the natural. However, before we shame the disciples, think of the times that you and I have tried to understand the Word of God through our natural sense and have miserably failed.

Jesus went continued to teach them a great lesson;

*"How is it that ye do not understand that I spake it not concerning bread, that ye should beware of the leaven of the Pharisees of the Sadducees?"*

*"Then understood they how that He bade them not of the leaven of bread, but of the doctrine of the Pharisees and of the Sadducees." Matthew 16:11-12*

You may be asking, *"How does this connect to faith or lack thereof?"* This is a great question, and the answer is found in verses nine through twelve. The disciples were looking and believing in the natural, what they could see, hear and understand within their own minds. They were showing how insensitive they were to the things of the Spirit. Not understanding spiritual things can be devastating. Understanding Spiritual things are paramount for the believer. With some of the teaching that is coming from the modern day church we desperately need Spiritual understanding, for, without it, deception is before us.

When Jesus questioned His disciples asking them: *"Do you yet not understand and neither remember?"* The question was; "Have you forgotten the miracle of the loaves and fishes.

The Palmist put it this way;

*"Through thy precepts I get understanding: therefore I hate every false way." Psalm 119:104*

*(This Stanza closes with the statement that wisdom which flows from Scriptures destroys all desire for false teaching) Source; The Expositors Study Bible Jimmy Swaggaqrt*

Satan would and is trying to make people think and believe that there are many roads to God, which is an outright lie!

> *"The thief cometh not, but for to steal, and to kill, and to destroy: (his destruction comes by the way of false teaching): I am come that they might have life, and that they might have it more abundantly." (Jesus Christ is the way to salvation and the ability to walk in the newness of life!)*

*See Romans chapters five, six, seven and eight.* These chapters include the *"Mechanics and Dynamics of the Holy Spirit,"* which is a must if you (we) are to walk in the victory that Jesus Christ has bought for us.

When true revelation of the Scriptures are known, not only does It raise an awareness of false teaching, it also makes clear the way for right living.

Contrary to some popular teaching, there is only one way for Salvation and that is through and by, **THE CROSS AND THE FINISHED WORK OF JESUS CHRIST!"**

It is a must that every believer walks in correct faith which is in the Cross and what Jesus Christ accomplished there. When our faith is put in something else we will fall prey to; *"O YE OF LITTLE FAITH!"*


## "O FAITHLESS GENERATION"

# CHAPTER 7

# "Lord, help my unbelief"

*"And straightway the father of the child cried
out, and with tears, Lord I believe;
help thou mine unbelief"
Mark 9:24*

This is one of my favorite passages of scripture to teach on. Jesus along with Peter, James and John was coming from one of the greatest experiences for the disciples and that was ***"The Mount of Transfiguration."*** It was such a great experience that Peter wanted to build three tabernacles, one for Jesus, one for Moses and one for Elijah. Upon leaving there, He along with Peter, James and John joined the other nine disciples who were in sort of a mess. He was met with a man in dyer straights.

*"And one of the multitude answered and said, Master, I have brought unto You my son spirit which has a dumb spirit." Mark 9:17*

The demon spirit kept the child from speaking and would torment his body even to the degree of trying to kill him.

> *"And wheresoever he (the demon spirit)* **takes him, he tears him:and he foams, and he gnashes with his teeth, and pines away: and I spoke to Your Disciples that they should cast him out; and they could not." Mark 9:18**

It appears the Disciples had tried time and time again to rid the child of the demon spirit without any success. The inability of the Disciples to cast out this demon spirit created a mess to say the least.

> *"He (Jesus) answered him, and said, O faithless generation, how long shall I be with you? How long shall I suffer you? Bring him to Me."*

**Jesus was asking; how long are you going to continue to walk in misplaced faith?**

> *"And they brought him unto Him: and when he (the demon spirit) saw Him Jesus) straightway (immediately) the spirit (demon spirit) tore him and fell on the ground, and wallowed foaming."*

> *"And He (Jesus) asked his father, How long is it since this came unto him? And he said, Of a child."*

Notice, how the demon spirit reacted when the boy was brought into the presence of Jesus Christ (v-20). Demonic powers cannot stand before the power of God!

*"And oftentimes it has cast him into the fire, and into waters, to destroy him (this was an extremely destructive spirit to the degree of trying to kill the boy) but if You can do anything have compassion on us, and help us."*

**The phrase;** *"but if You can do anything; reveals the father was not settled in faith in what Jesus Christ could do. I do believe that the father was unsettled do to the failures of the disciples to deliver his son.*

*"Jesus Said unto him, If you can believe, all things are possible to him who believes"*

There are two very important points in the above scripture;

1. **If our object of faith is right nothing is impossible!**

2. **If God promised it, you can have it!**

**The word believe is from the Greek word, 'Pisteuo' from 'pistis' meaning; faith; to believe, give credit to. Be mentally persuaded, be of an opinion; to believe in or on Christ Jesus implying, knowledge (knowing with confidence) to have confident in.**

*"And straightway the father of the child cried out and said with tears, Lord, I believe help Thou mine unbelief."*

The phrase *"help Thou mine unbelief"* is from the Greek, meaning; faithlessness, or uncertainty; lacking confidence in the Power of Jesus Christ. In general it is a lack of trust on or in the God of promise.

Upon hearing the Words of Jesus, the father **'immediately'** cried out with tears. This cry came from deep within and being full of hope! Notice; within this father dwelt, belief and unbelief. How can that be? I really believed what certain that he really believed what Jesus said to him. However, with the failures of the disciples it left him without being totally convinced. Notice a couple of things here;

1. *"Lord I believe"* **proclaims belief howbeit, insufficient, for it was** *'Misplaced faith.'* It is very possible that his faith was in the disciples to deliver his son which again would have been *'Misplaced Faith!'*

2. *"Help Mine unbelief"* is a cry for help to understand how to receive what Jesus was saying; *"All things are possible to him who believes." The belief (Faith) has to have to correct object which is the Cross and the finished work of Jesus Christ.* The father of this child had to remove his faith from focusing on the disciples and focusing on Jesus Christ.

I am certain that there are thousands, if not tens of thousands of Christians today who are struggling not knowing how to walk in the *'Newness of Life' (Romans 6) and the 'Victory that Jesus Christ won at Calvary.'* **MANY ARE WALKING IN MISPLACED FAITH!"**

**WHEN THE OBJECT OF YOUR FAITH IS RIGHT THE OUTCOME WILL BE RIGHT!**

# CHAPTER 8

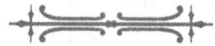

# "You did run well"

### "Where Has Our Faith Gone?

It is believed that the Apostle Paul visited the Church of Galatia in his second and third missionary journeys (Acts 16:6; 18:23). While visiting there Paul established that Salvation alone is through the *'Cross and the Finished Work of Jesus Christ.'* Thus, the believers faith was established in the *'Cross and the Finished Work of Jesus Christ.'*

In Paul's absence, teachers came in from Palestine called, *"Judaizers."* They began to teach and insist that these could not be true Christians unless they submitted themselves to the Jewish ordinance of circumcision. They accepted this teaching without hesitation, just as they did with the teaching of the Apostle Paul. They also taught that the believers there must adhere to the "Law of Moses." This misguided false teaching created **'Misplaced Faith'** in the believers of Galtia.

This prompted Paul to write this letter. The main purpose of this letter was to come against the heresy of the Judaizers teaching that the work of Jesus Christ was not sufficient enough for Salvation. Paul also brought attention to his authenticity of being an Apostle. Paul revealed that he was equal to the original apostles because he had received his doctrine straight from Jesus Christ through revelation (Gal. 1:11-19)

Once Paul had established his apostleship, he then proved that men are justified by faith in the *'Cross and the Finished Work of Jesus Christ,'* rather than works of the Law. Paul's teaching continued with the establishing a life being led by the Holy Spirit (Gal. 5:16- 6:10).

Within rebuking the teaching of the Judaizsers and reestablishing faith in the *'Cross and the Finished Work of Jesus Christ,'* Paul presented the Galatians with some in-depth questions teaching or lack thereof of the Modern Day Church.

> *"O foolish Galatians (their foolishness was due to their total lack of perception of the falsehood of the Judaizers doctrine) who has bewitched you (who has influenced you so that you would Misplace your Faith?) not to obey the truth (took your eyes off of the Cross and what Jesus Christ accomplished there), before whose eyes Jesus Christ has been evidently set forth, crucified among you?(the Apostle Paul Preached the Cross and what Jesus Christ Finished there with such clarity, that there should not be any doubt concern the object of faith).*

*"This only would I learn of you (Paul is going to reveal the error using the following question), Did you receive the Spirit by works of the Law, or by the hearing of faith?" (how were you "Born Again," by your own works of by your faith in the Cross and the Finished Work of Jesus Christ?)*

*"Are you so foolish? (give this some serious thought) having begun in the Spirit (since you were "Born Again" by your faith in Jesus Christ, do you really that you can now reach spiritual maturity within your own works?), are you now made perfect by the flesh (How is it that you received Salvation through Faith and now think that you can progress in Sanctification by your own self efforts and ability?) Galatians 3:1-3*

*"You did run well (you were staying on the right path) who did hinder you (who or what got In your path) that you should not obey the truth (why did you continue listening to false teachers who led you astray [away from the Cross and what Jesus Christ Finished].*

*"This persuasion (teaching on works to gain Salvation and Sanctification) comes not from Him (the Holy Spirit) Who calls you (think about what you are doing, it is not biblically corrorect). Galatians 5:7-8*

What grieves me is, the '**Modern Day**' church has given into this same kind of trap and that is sugar coating, water down, trying to become culturally relevant that sight has been lost concerning the **"Cross and the Finished Work of Jesus Christ."** The **'Modern Day'** church is doing a great job of making people feel good without making them good (without an inward transformation into the **"Image of Jesus Christ."**

The Modern Day Church is drowning in grace living any way they please without a sin conscience. The Name it Claim group has caused devastation in many lives. Others have put works in front of faith while others are working to build huge campuses rather than building lives. We cannot fall for the deception that is in our Church world today.

Notice the warning that the Apostle Paul gave to a young evangelist named Timothy:

> *"This know also, that in the last days (the days in which we now live) perilous times shall come (this is speaking of difficult dangerous times, which Christians living just before the Rapture encounter).*
>
> *"For men (those who call themselves Christians) shall be lovers of their own selves, covetous, boasters, proud, blasphemers, disobedient to parents, unthankful, unholy,*
>
> *"Without natural affection, trucebreakers, false accusers, incontinent despise, fierce, despisers of those who are good,*
>
> *"Traitors, heady, highminded, lovers of pleasures more than lovers of God (and remember, this is*

*describing the Endtime Church, which has been totally corrupted [Matt. 13:33; Rev. 3:14-22]);*

*"Having a form of Godliness (refers to all the trappings of Christianity, but without power), but denying the power thereof (the modern Church, for all its practical purposes, has denied the Cross; in doing this, they have denied that through which the Holy Spirit works, and in Whom the power resides [Rom. 8:1-2,11; 1 Cor. 1:18]): from such turn away. (No half measures are to be adopted here. The command is clear! It means to turn away from Churches that deny the Cross). 2 Tim. 3:1-5 The Expositor's Study Bible Jimmy Swaggart*

I believe that it is crystal clear that we are on the brink (maybe the church already has) of falling into the state of Apostasy! Therefore, we must not waver nor shrink back in our faith in the **'Cross and the Finished Work of Jesus Christ!'**

**See; Hebrews 10:23; 35-39 James never put works ahead of faith!**

# CHAPTER 9

# "Where Has Our Faith Gone?

(The Faith Message)

The question within the **"Modern Day Church"** is, **"Where has our faith gone?"** I am concerned that more faith has been placed in multi-millionaire preachers, living in luxurious mansions which have become self-seekers. Please understand, I am certainly not against those who carry the True Gospel from being worthy of their labor. However, I am opposed to those who are living such lives that they have need of nothing and are preying on people to continue them in their riches. It certainly is not wrong to have your favorite preacher and support them when they are preaching and teaching the truth of the Word. However, the line is crossed for me when believers began to worship those preachers and teachers. The Modern Day Church seems to be more about money, numbers and huge buildings rather than the building of lives within the Kingdom.

Before I go any further me say; I believe that within our (tongue) mouth is the **'Power of life and death' (Prov. 18:21).** I believe that within our words we are **'justified or condemned'** **(Matt. 12:37).** I believe that if we do not **'allow doubt to enter our hearts we shall receive what we say.'** I also believe that **'whatsoever you desire when you pray believe that you receive them, you shall have them.' (Mark 11:23-24).** However, my object of Faith concerning all of these things is in **'The Cross and the finished Work of Jesus Christ!'**

I am not saying it is wrong to have trust and to support those preaching the Gospel. However, when our faith is placed upon the individual preacher/teacher more so than upon Jesus Christ, we have a huge problem. I personally know of families who have put their faith and trust in what some rich preacher is teaching only to be devastated. When the so-called **'Faith Message'** came to the forefront many bought into the confession, name it, claim it doctrine and when you see those same people today, they are still confessing, still naming it, and still claiming it with no results. That is because they have placed their faith in what they are saying rather than in the **'Cross and the finished Work of Jesus Christ!'** What good is quoting scripture without partaking within the scripture? So, often, these things have become more **'work oriented than faith based.'** Therein is a great problem. It becomes, **'Misplaced Faith.'**

**Many believers have been led astray by teaching scripture out of context. Let's examine some of the following examples;**

> *"Cast your bread upon the waters: for shall find it after many days." Eccl. 11:1*

This scripture is speaking of God giving a Promise with every Promise being fulfilled. Even though days, weeks and months may go by we are not to grow weary and not lose faith (Eccl.11:3-4). The concern that I have is; I have often heard this scripture taught on in the concept of money. Matter a fact, there is a quote in a song that is even more troubling; *'Cast your bread upon the waters and it shall come back to you on very wave, pressed down shaken down and running over.''* I have searched the Hebrew meaning of the word, *'Bread'* can't find anywhere it is speaking of money Could this principle of seed sowing apply here? It is very possible. However, to plant the thought, that if we (you) give (sow) money into a particular ministry and it will come back to us on every wave is somewhat out of bounds. First, the scripture doesn't say anything about what we so coming back on every wave. God has never promised to make everyone millionaires. Please don' misunderstand what I am saying; I firmly believe we have an obligation to support where we are getting our spiritual food. However, it cannot be with the idea of becoming rich! Secondly, where is our faith? Is it upon the waves returning or is it upon the *'Cross and the Finished Work of Jesus Christ?'*

> *"Give and it shall be given unto you good measure, pressed down, and shaken together, and running over shall men give unto your bosom. For with the same measure that you mete withal shall be measured to you again."*
> *Luke 6:38*

Here again, is a passage of scripture often used when receiving an offering or teaching on sowing money. Before I give you my concerning, may I say, the *'Law of Reciprocity.'* However, context (subject) of this scripture is rarely taught. Notice in verse 37; it is speaking of not judging nor condemning and the extension of *'forgiving'* that we may be *'forgiven.'*

The problem here is, expecting a financial overflow and yet not addressing the subject matter. An un-forgiving heart can lead to this message becoming one of greed. So, am I saying it is wrong to give money and not expect money in return? No, I am not saying that at all. I am saying, the context (the subject) needs to be taught. If you want to use it as a principle of the *'Law of Reciprocity'* fine, but be sure everyone hearing understands what the passage is saying. As important as money is, it is not everything!

> *"(As it is written, I (God) have made you a father of many nations (referring to Abraham, Gen. 12:1-3; 17:4-5) before Him Whom (God) he (Abraham) believed, even God, who quickens the dead (brings to life that which is dead (referring to the deadness of Sarah's womb), and calls those things which be not as though they were. Romans 4:17*

I love this passage of scripture. What a promise God made to Abraham, who continued to believe God even when in the natural he was facing no hope (Romans 4:18-17). But, there is something very important to take notice of here. **It is God Who is calling those things which be as there were!**

I have personally witnessed believers trying to call things into existence based on this scripture. Her is something we must understand; **If God calls it in His Word than we (you) can call it; however, if God hasn't called it we (you) are wasting our breath. IT WILL NOT HAPPEN!**

*"Be not deceived (the Galatians had fallen prey to false teaching, which can happen and is happening today) God is not mocked (mocking God is when anything is put between you and Him, especially, when it comes to the Cross and what Jesus Christ accomplished or there, for the is no substitute) for whatsoever a man sows, that shall he also reap (once again, this is speaking of the 'Law of Reciprocity,' man will reap whatever it is he sows).*

*"For he who sows to his flesh shall of the flesh reap corruption (this is speaking osper[more specifically the Apostle Paul was addressing the works that were taugth by false teachers in order to receive salvation]but he who sows to the Spirit (speaking of the proper order of faith and that is the Cross and the Finished Work of Jesus Christ shall of the Spirit reap life everlasting. Gal. 6:7-8*

I have also heard this passage used sowing money. Is money more important than the **involved here, however let's keep things in proper context!**

Another One;

*"Beloved, I wish (pray) above all things that thou mayest prosper and be in health, even as thy soul shall prosper." 3 John 2*

There are some who misplay this verse to mean that God's will for His children is to always prosper and be in health, which gives credence to the belief in a "health and wealth gospel."

However, the writer is conveying nothing more than a wish to Gaius that this letter might find him in good health.

There are several words in this verse mistranslated in the KJV. For instance ,(the phrase *"above all things")* the preposition *'peri'* should be rendered "concerning" or "about" rather than "above." John is not stating that prosperity and wealth should be important priorities in one's life. The idea of mere wishing is expressed by the verb *'euchomai,"* not of a promise given by an Apostle to a fellow believer. The word translated *"prosper" is "euodousthai'* (a present infinitive from *"euodoo."* Essentially, this word means to have a good and safe journey Lifebenevolence toward Christians. Although it is translated........*"as God hath prospered him.......,"* one should accept the idea that prospering necessarily means to gain material needs, and the idea of wealth should not be interpreted here. The third word of importance in this verse is *"hugianein" "to be healthy."* Likewise, this is not a guarantee that Gaius is going to be healthy, but simply expresses a wish. Hebrew Greek Study Bible

It is totally not scriptural to even think that the measure of a successful Christian life is based on what he/she posses. It is certainly not wrong to have possessions in this life. However, when they are exploited above the Cross and what Jesus Christ did there, it is not only wrong, it is sin! Christ's death, burial and resurrection was to eradicate sin and take away the dominion of man's sin nature bringing the believer into the **'Newness of Life' (Rom. 6)** and bring into existence the **'Law of the Spirit of Life' (Rom. 8)** when the believer walks in these he/she will discover **God's Prescribed Order of Victory!**

One more and this one is really fascinating to me, believers confessing; **"money cometh."** It will if you get a job and invest your money properly! No! I am not against money whatsoever. My issue is when teachers are using such scriptures to get people to give while they (the teacher) become millionaires while the giver is poorer than Job's turkey (if Job had a turkey). There are thousands who have allowed bondage in their life because of wrong teaching. Or, may I say, teaching without clarity. Is one so gullible, that they think just saying, **"money cometh"** will put money into their bank account? Come on, let's get real!

The Apostle Paul instructed a young evangelist by the name of Timothy to keep things in proper order.

> *"Study to show thyself approved unto God, a workman that needth not to be ashamed rightly dividing the Word of Truth." 2 Tim. 2:15*

## WE MUST DO THE SAME!

## IF THE BELIEVER WILL KEEP THE CROSS AND THE FINISHED WORK OF JESUS CHRIST THE OBJECT OF THEIR FAITH EVERYTHING WILL WORK OUT ACCORDING TO GOD'S PURPOSE AND THAT INCLUDES FINANCES! ROMANS 8:28

### Don't Be Lead Astray By Unbiblical Teaching!

# CHAPTER 10

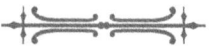

# "The Only Way to Live in Correct Faith"

**Hebrews 12:2; Luke 9:23**

Without being redundant, let me begin by repeating God's plan for the *'Correct Object of Our Faith'* from chapter one.

On the sixth day, God created the greatest of all His creation, He created man in His own image and likeness; male and female. He blessed them and gave them the ability to be fruitful, and to multiply, and to replenish the earth. He gave them dominion over all the inhabitants of the earth. God gave them every herb bearing seed, and every tree yielding seed for meat with the exception of the Tree of Knowledge of Good and Evil. His command was;

> *"But of the Tree of the Knowledge of Good and Evil, you shall not eat of it for in the day that you eat thereof you shall surely die. Gen. 2:17*

The day came when Eve was approached by the serpent, who, was being used by Satan. He said to Eve;

> *"Now the serpent was more subtle than any beast of the field which the Lord God had made. And he said unto the woman, Yes, has God said, You shall not eat of every tree of the Garden?"*

> *"And the woman said unto the serpent, We may eat of the trees of the Garden."*

> *"But of the fruit of the tree which is in the midst of the garden, God said, You shall not eat of it, neither shall you touch it, lest you die." Gen. 3:1-3*

In Eve's response she added to what God had spoken to Adam. God never said, *'neither shall you touch the tree.'* Any time we add too or take away from what God has spoken we become vulnerable to the onslaught of the enemy. Notice in verses 4 and 5 the endless pursuit of the serpent to deceive Eve. Satan outright denies the Word of God before Eve.

When Eve saw that the tree was good for food, and it was pleasant to her eyes, she partook of it and gave Adam some and he did eat. This was the very beginning of the three temptations; *"the lust of the flesh, lust of the eyes, and the pride of life."* Even from these, one cannot excuse Adam. While Eve was deceived and submitted to temptation Adam was not. He blatantly disregarded what God had spoken to Him. Adam's sin was not partaking of the tree of Knowledge of Good and Evil. Adam's sin was due to unbelief; he just did not believe what God had said to him. It was his unbelief that led to his disobedience. This was the beginning of **'Misplaced Faith!'**

59

Adam placed his faith within his own strength, ability and knowledge. This is amazing considering the time that Adam spent with God. Nobody knows how long it was from the time Adam was created until he fell. The reason being, Adam was created an eternal so there was no need for time.

The feeble attempt of Adam and Eve sewing together fig leaves and making themselves aprons in order to cover their nakedness (sin) was insufficient at best. It is like the sinner of toady who tries to cover themselves with, self made morality and religious practices. Again, this was because of Adam **'Misplacing his Faith!'**

## God Revealed What Must Be the Object of Faith!

## The Promise of the Cross and the Finished Work of Jesus Christ!

> *"And I will put enmity (animosity) between you and the woman (presents the Lord now "You used the woman to bring down the human race, and I will use the woman as an instrument to bring the Redeemer into the world, Who will save human race), and between your seed (mankind which follows Satan) and her Seed (the Lord Jesus Christ); it (Christ) shall bruise your head (the Victory that Jesus won at the Cross [Col. 2:14-15]), and you shall bruise His Heel (the sufferings of the Cross). Gen. 3:15 21 Expositor's Study Bible Jimmy Swaggart*

From this time forward, the object of man's faith had to be focused on the coming Messiah, Jesus Christ and what He would accomplish on the Cross. While waiting on the coming Christ there had to be blood sacrifices made of animals. Even though these sacrifices could not deliver man nor take care of his sin problem. Yet, these sacrifices pointed to the Supreme Sacrifice and that being Jesus Christ (Hebrews 10:1-18)!

Notice the following scripture;

> *"Looking unto Jesus the Author and Finisher of our Faith; Who for the joy that was set before Him endured the Cross, despising the shame, and is set down at the Right Hand of the Throne of God." Hebrews 12:2*

With so many distractions in this world it is understandable how difficult it may be at times to continue *"Looking unto Jesus."* Well, I am convinced beyond any doubt that Jesus Christ gave us the answer that will cause us to look beyond the distractions of this world and keep our Faith Focused on Him!

The believer will never have to be concerned with **'Misplacing their Faith'** if they will follow the instructions of Jesus recorded in Luke 9:23

> *"And He said to them all, if any man will come after me, let him deny himself, and take up his cross daily, and follow me." Luke 9:23*

Let's examine this great passage of scripture closely;

The *Phrase, "And He said to them all" what Jesus was about to speak included anyone and everyone that would hear his teaching. Meaning, no one is exempt from the following!* Jesus

61

Christ is the only way to Salvation and no man can come unto the Father except through Him.

> *"Jesus saith unto him, I am the way, the truth, and the life: no man cometh unto the Father but by me." John 14:6*

Anyone coming to Jesus Christ for Salvation must confess and believe in the *"Cross and the Finished Work of Jesus Christ.*

> *"That if thou shalt confess with thy mouth the Lord Jesus, and shalt believe in thine heart that God raised Him from the dead, thou shalt be saved."*

> *"For with the heart man believeth unto righteousness; and with the mouth confession is made unto salvation."*

The Next thing that Jesus was proclaiming is the criteria for discipleship. This criteria includes everyone without exemption.

> *"Then said Jesus to those Jews which believed on Him, If ye continue in my Word, then are ye my disciples indeed." John 8:31*

The *Phrase, "Let Him"* this is not a request but rather a command. This is written grammatically in aorist imperative; which demands a command for doing something in the future that is a simple action. That action in the future is when one seeks Jesus Christ for Salvation. It is also written in the passive voice; representing the subject as receiving the action. Once again, this is all inclusive. Anyone coming to Jesus Christ must abide and live within the following criteria.

The *Phrase, "Deny himself"* is from the Greek word; *"Aparneomia"* meaning; to remove oneself, refuse, deny, disown. This word occurs only once and is a personal objective, which means to decline or withdraw from fellowship with anyone or anything. It denotes to give oneself. This is not asceticism as many think, but rather that a person denies their own ability and self-will, totally dependent on Jesus Christ and what He accomplished on the Cross. In other words, we are to stop trying to live for Jesus Christ within our own fleshly abilities. (Gal.3:1-3) There must be an avoidance of all forms of indulgence typically for religious reasons.

The believer is also to not be conformed to this world;

> *"I beseech you therefore, brethren, by the mercies of God, That ye present (place yourself in a position of a God opportunity) your bodies a living sacrifice, holy, acceptable unto God, which is your reasonable service."*

> *"And be not conformed (fashioned after) to this world: but be ye transformed (a transformation of quality for a qualitative new use) by the renewing of your mind, that ye may prove what is that good, and acceptable, and perfect, will of God." Romans 12:1-2*

The *Phrase, "Take up his cross daily"*

A. **The phrase, 'take up'** is a command for doing something in the future, the action, and aim. This is something that every believer must do.

B. **The Phrase, "His cross;" notice whose cross Jesus is speaking of;** it is the subjects (believers) cross i.e. those who come to Jesus Christ. The cross of o mean; Jesus Christ has two important elements; 1. Suffering 2. Victory. The cross the believer is to take up is looking exclusively to what Jesus Christ did at Calvary, i.e. meeting our every need. We are to take up the benefits of the '**Victory Jesus Won!' Of which I am still learning about daily!**

Over the years I have heard teaching on '**taking up your'** to mean, to carry a heavy load. I heard many believers say, '**my cross is jut to heavy to bare.'** May I say, you are carrying the wrong cross! Jesus Said;

> *"Come unto me, all ye that labor and are heavy laden, and I will give you rest."*
>
> *"Take my yoke upon you, and learn of me; for I am meek and lowly in heart: and ye shall find rest unto your souls."*
>
> *"For my yoke is easy, and my burden is light (meaning, sin and the punishment of it) Matt. 11:28-30*

The question is, why would Jesus lift from you and I the labor, the heavy laden, the exchanging of yokes and burdens, and then have us bare a cross that is too heavy?

The answer is, He doesn't place an unbearable cross on anyone, if it is too heavy for you than something is wrong. You just might be trying to carrying it within your own strength and ability which you were to deny yourself of.

Taking up your (our) cross is to begin to live in the benefits of the *'Cross and the Finished Work of Jesus Christ!'* In the great Gospel of John chapter nineteen verse thirty-three, Jesus proclaimed, *"It is Finished!"* From this point forward, the believer is to look exclusively to the *'Cross' which is the "Means' and to 'Jesus Christ' which is the 'Source'* of our every need! (Hebrews 12:2)

Jesus said, *"I am come that they might have life, and that they might have it more abundantly." John 10:10b (Romans 6, 8)*

He also said, *"In this world you shall have tribulation, but be of good cheer I have overcome the world." John 16:33b*

The Apostle Paul in his revelation of the *'Cross and what Jesus Christ did there'* made the following statement;

> *"I am crucified with Christ; nevertheless I live; yet not I, but Christ liveth in me: and the life which I now live in the flesh I live by the faith of the Son of God, who loved me, and gave himself for me." Galatians 2:20*

**Living that crucified life is recorded in Romans chapters 6, 7 and 8!**

**The Cross and Discipleship;**

1. **The believer reckons and counts himself crucified with Christ. Romans 6:11; Galatians 2:20; 5:24**

2.  The believer reckons and counts himself dead to sin once and for always, but, alive in Christ. Romans 6:11; 1 Peter 4:2

3.  The believer does not allow sin to reign in his body. Romans 6:12,14; Colossians 3:5

4.  The Believer does not yield the parts of his body to sin, as an instrument of wickedness. Romans 6:13; 8:13

5.  The believer yields himself to Jesus Christ. Roman 6:13b; 12:1-2; 13:14

6.  The believer yields his body as instruments of righteousness. Romans 6:13c; Romans 8; Galatians 5:16

7.  The believer will mortify the deeds of his body. Romans 8:13

The believer is to take up his cross **'daily;'** this is an extremely important command. It is given with the idea of looking to the **'Cross;'** renewing their faith on a daily basis for what Jesus Christ did at the Cross i.e. **'His Finished Work!'**

Daily, the believer is to walk in the benefits of the Cross and what Jesus Christ did there. The believer must resist the enemy from removing them from the **'Cross being the object of their faith!'**

The *Phrase, "And follow Me"* is written as an imperative verb which commands a continuous and repeated action. Christ can only be followed as long as the believer has his object of faith in the **'Cross and the Finished Work of Jesus Christ'** with an understanding (revelation) of what He accomplished there, and by that means only. Romans 6:3-5, 11, 14; 8:1-2, 11; 1Corinthians 1:17-18, 21, 23; Galatians 6:14; Ephesians 2:13-19; Colossians 2:14-15. To live this life following Jesus Christ daily must be a walk under the direction and leading of the Holy Spirit. Romans 8

## Jesus Christ has destroyed the Enemy!

*"Blotting out the handwriting of ordinances*
*that was against, which was contrary to us,*
*and took it out of the way,*
*nailing it to His cross."*

*"And having spoiled, principalities,*
*and powers, He made a show of them openly,*
*triumphing over them in it (in the Cross)."*
*Colossians 2:14-15*

*"For whatsoever is born of God overcometh*
*the world: and this is the victory that*
*overcometh the world even our faith."*
*1 John 5:4*

## IT IS FINIFHED, JOHN 19:30

## THE NEWNESS OF LIFE IS NOW AVAILABLE TO YOU!!!

# ABOUT THE AUTHOR

Dr. Baldock is the founder/president of *"Gaining The Victory Ministries."* He is currently in his fifteth year of ministry.

Dr. Baldock began his ministry in March of 1971. In March of 1973, he began in full time ministry. He and his wife Julie have been married for thirty-five years. Together they have seven grown children, Rick, Tammy, Tracy, Rhonda, Alicia, Michael and Ashley. He and Julie also have several grandchildren and great-grandchildren.

Dr. Baldock has pastored nine churches; four of which he pioneered and built from the ground floor up. Dr. Baldock also has four earned Doctorate Degrees, and one Honorary Doctorate.

He is currently traveling around to different Churches teaching and preaching the word of God. He now attends the Sanctuary Church in Beech Grove/ Indianapolis, Indianan. Dr. Baldock has spoke at many conventions and has worked with several well known ministries. He taught for several years with the International College of Bible Theology and with Midwest Seminary. He has taught undergraduate and graduate school. He taught at the School of the Prophets in Poplar Bluff, Missouri for about four years, and he taught about two to three years at The Lion of Judah in Malden, Missouri.

Dr. Baldock also traveled to Malawi in East Africa and, for thirteen days he, and two other ministers trained over one hundred and twenty-five church leaders.

Dr. Baldock is a gifted preacher and teacher of the Word. He has authored many books and study helps. He believes that the gifts that God has given him should be shared and imparted to others. He believes that everyday, practical teaching will reveal the application of the Word of God in the person's everyday living. He is a strong believer in the fact that everything you will ever receive from God is because of the **"Cross"** and **"The finished work of Jesus Christ."**

He believes that the **"Cross"** is the means of all you will ever need, and that **"Jesus Christ is the Source"** of all God has supplied for us.

Dr. Baldock is available to speak and teach at your local church or, conferences, along with leadership training and motivational speaking. If you would like for Dr. Baldock to come and speak at your church or conference, and if you would like more information about his books, CD's, DVD's and a plethora of teaching tools, you can write to:

Gaining the Victory Ministries, Inc.
Dr. Mike Baldock
P.O. Box 648
Spencer, Indian 47460
Or, you can e-mail him at;
gainingvictoryministries@gmail.com

CPSIA information can be obtained
at www.ICGtesting.com
Printed in the USA
LVHW032228250521
688475LV00005B/246